Dedicated to Noriaki Yuasa, Niisan Takahashi, and Shunsuke Kikuchi for still doing their best even with a crappy deal.

THE UNOFFICIAL TOKUSATSU FAN'S HANDBOOK FOR GAMERA, SUPER MONSTER

宇宙怪獣ガメラ

by Constantine Furman

THE UNOFFICIAL TOKUSATSU FAN'S HANDBOOK FOR *GAMERA, SUPER MONSTER*

ISBN-10: B097VBGYTL
ISBN-13: 9798522013776

Front cover art by Andre Dubois.
Back cover art by Luis Quijano, www.instagram.com/ominoso1984/

Special thanks to my pal Matt Ferrett of www.monstersconquertheuniverse.com for allowing me to ~~steal~~ use some of his fine jokes and observations. His review of *Gamera, Super Monster* at his site is the fairest one I've ever encountered.
Special thanks to Andre Dubois and Luis Quijano for allowing the usage of their beautiful art pieces.

TABLE OF CONTENTS

FOREWORD

Why *Gamera, Super Monster*? Because nobody else cares about it, that's why. Do you care? Maybe a little, but probably not enough to attempt to clear the air about it.

Arrow Video didn't care about this particular title and they had the perfect opportunity to truly educate Gamera fans about it. However, they didn't double-check the audio commentary recorded for *Super Monster* because it is full of the same old misinformation that populates the internet and gets regurgitated by everyone else talking about the movie, plus a bunch of half-assed assumptions based on cynicism verging on malice. On top of that, Arrow couldn't be bothered to find someone who didn't have searing contempt for Gamera himself to speak on the movie's behalf (did no one think to call Mach Fumiake?). Call me crazy, but a prerequisite to doing an audio commentary should be that you can at least tolerate the subject matter you're speaking about.

This book—as far as I know—is the first ever of its kind: a literary audio commentary. The comments and information I have gleamed from my extensive research are attached to a timecode that can be used while watching the movie to follow along with. It is meant to be an antidote to the commentary Arrow allowed on their release. It will require you to both read and listen/watch the movie at the same time, but I'd bet dollars to donuts that you can do it.

If you managed to make it through Arrow's *Gamera, Super Monster* audio commentary, you owe it to yourself to read this book, chiefly because you have been mislead everywhere else. These are the facts as I have been able to discern them from sources on both sides of the Pacific and with an open mind to what the facts of the matter may have been.

It is my devout hope by the time you get to the end, you will have learned something interesting about this least cared-about of Gamera's illustrious exploits. Because I love this movie and it's nowhere near as bad as everyone acts like it is.

And it's way past time that *Gamera, Super Monster* got its due.

CHAPTER ONE

IN THE BEGINNING,
THERE WAS GAMERA...
AND IT WAS GOOD.

Daiei Motion Picture Company was the second biggest film studio in Japan after Toho Company, LTD. However, it was Daiei who first broke Japanese cinema into the rest of the world with the release of Akira Kurosawa's *Rashomon* (1952). Kurosawa would soon afterward move over to Toho and have an incredibly successful run with them.

Daiei is a combination of the Japanese words "dai" which means "big" or "great" and "ei" taken from "eiga," which means "movie." Their output was very popular with moviegoers, especially after the release of *A Tale of Zatoichi* (1962) starring Shintaro Katsu. Daiei's Zatoichi proved so popular that he would return in dozens of sequels.

By the mid-60s, with the help of the dream team of director Ishiro Honda and special effects wizard Eiji Tsuburaya, Toho had cornered the market in the extremely successful (and lucrative) kaiju eiga ("monster movie") genre. The heads of Daiei decided they needed to get in on that action. They had made a sort-of monster movie in 1962 called *The Whale God* starring Kojiro Hongo and Shintaro Katsu. But it's hardly a monster movie and more of a jidaigeki ("historical drama"). Their first attempt at a bona fide monster movie concerned a swarm of giant rats, *Giant Horde Beast Nezura.* For some reason, the effects people thought they could get away with using actual rats in miniature cities. When fleas from the rats infested the studio, production on *Nezura* was shut down and eventually cancelled altogether.

Still having the itch for kaiju eiga, so to speak, Daiei started production on a new film. The screenplay was turned in as *Fire-Breathing Turtle Attacks Tokyo* but would eventually be released as the far-less cumbersome *Giant Monster Gamera*. Since none of Daiei's big directors would touch the project, it was handed over to fledgling director Noriaki Yuasa, whose previous movie had bombed at the box office.

Yuasa worked his hardest to make as good a movie as he could with the limitations he had but when the finished film was screened for the Daiei brass, the executives said "Well, that's how it is, sometimes." But president of Daiei Masaichi Nagata confusingly asked "Isn't it good?" which immediately caused all the executives to back peddle and agree they loved it too.

Nagata wasn't alone; *Gamera* turned out to be a huge hit for Daiei when it was released in late November of 1965 (just a month or so before Toho's *Monster Zero* hit screens). Children loved this new flying turtle monster. Naturally, a sequel was rushed into production but Noriaki Yuasa wasn't asked back to direct. Instead, house director Shigeo Tanaka was assigned the project. Yuasa was, however, allowed to direct the special effects sequences. The first thing Tanaka decreed was "no kids," absolutely missing what had made *Gamera* a hit with its target audience in the first place. Instead, Tanaka aimed his movie squarely at adults and rather than a wild-and-woolly monster movie like *Gamera* had been, his movie was more of a dramatic morality play about the vice of greed where the monsters took a back seat.

The resultant movie, *Gamera vs. Barugon*, opened on a double bill with another Daiei monster movie,

Majin (*Majin* had been produced at the Kyoto branch of Daiei, while the Gamera movies were made at the Tokyo branch). While *Majin* was a success (spawning two sequels later that same year!), *Barugon* was not, especially with children, who found the movie boring and would run up and down the theater aisles until the monsters appeared onscreen.

Daiei decided to make another Gamera picture, but this time Yuasa was back in the director's chair for both the human and special effects scenes. This time, however, everything seemed to gel and 1967's *Gamera vs. Gaos* managed to become the most successful Japanese monster movie of the year (beating out Shochiku's *The X From Outer Space*, Nikkatsu's *Gappa, the Triphibian Monster*, Toei's Korean co-production *Yongary, Monster from the Deep*, and Toho's duo of *King Kong Escapes* and *Son of Godzilla*).

At first, seen as just a "Godzilla rip-off," but three movies in and Gamera was already a serious rival to the King of the Monsters at the box office. Budgetarily-speaking, the series' fourth entry, *Gamera vs. Viras*, was more successful than Toho's *Destroy All Monsters* in 1968 and 1969's *Gamera vs. Guiron* was more successful than *Godzilla's Revenge*, the first real attempt by Toho to win back some of the audience Daiei had managed to snatch away from Godzilla. 1970's *Gamera vs. Jiger* went on to become the most successful Gamera film yet.

However, Daiei was being completely mismanaged and instead of putting the movies' profits back into future productions as they're supposed to, that money went to political contributions and other shady shenanigans. Movies like *Gamera vs. Viras* and *Gamera vs. Guiron* could have had more money spent on them; the Daiei brass merely chose not to in favor of their own selfish ends. Eventually, however, the bottom fell out and Daiei found itself lacking in funds. Despite their hugely successful output (Zatoichi was on his 20th movie at this point!), Daiei was bankrupt and instead of announcing that publicly and letting its employees know, the brass decided to hide it in hopes they could overcome it.

The seventh movie, *Gamera vs. Zigra*, was produced during this period and it's a miracle the movie was even completed. The seams started to show of Daiei's secret bankruptcy when Daiei couldn't even release *Zigra* domestically, instead handing it over to Dainichi Films for distribution in Japan. There is no real data on how well the movie did because it didn't even matter. Daiei's employees weren't being paid and were working for promised deferred payments. In December of 1971, Daiei finally announced publicly that it was bankrupt and would be halting film production.

Realizing they had been working all this time for nothing, Daiei's [ex]employees raided the film studio and furiously destroyed everything they could get their hands on. This included the Gamera suit and miniature props. This is why there are only a finite amount of publicity stills and posters for Daiei's films now: they are all that could be saved by filmmakers like Noriaki Yuasa, braving the riot to save anything they could get their hands on. This is also why there are no props leftover from the Gamera movies today.

And this is why the only surviving print of *Gamera vs. Gaos* has frame damage during the final battle and the negative of the 90-minute version of *Gamera vs. Viras* is lost.

Since Daiei was putting on a facade of business as usual, after *Gamera vs. Zigra* was completed, plans were set in motion for an eighth Gamera movie for 1972. The contracts were signed for the series' regulars and work began on the film, concerning a two-headed monster named Wyvern. Noriaki Yuasa claimed the suit was built, even though no script was written, but it was certainly destroyed in the riot.

Daiei was dead. Noriaki Yuasa moved into television, where he managed to carve out a successful niche for himself. In 1974, Tokuma Publishing would buy up Daiei and all their properties (they could not get Zatoichi, however, as Shintaro Katsu had successfully moved him over to Toho and continued the series there). Yasuyoshi Tokuma produced a few movies here and there under the Daiei banner, but a movie's producer is who its money comes from. There was no Daiei and there was no Daiei funds, so Tokuma Publishing were the true producers of these movies.

By the late 70s, Tokuma discovered the signed contracts for the eighth Gamera movie that never was and called them in. The contracts were signed with Daiei, but since Tokuma owned everything that Daiei owned, Yasuyoshi Tokuma felt those contracts now applied to them. Normally, Noriaki Yuasa would have loved the chance to be making Gamera movies again, but bizarrely, Tokuma was not giving him an appropriate budget to do so. "Tokuma didn't want to take much of a risk," Yuasa would explain in interviews later. When the director balked that a Gamera movie couldn't be made with the paltry budget Tokuma was giving him, the publishing giant dismissed him by telling him "We own everything. Use the old footage."

The eighth Gamera movie—such that it was—*Space Monster Gamera*, titled as such to cash in [rip-off] on *Space Battleship Yamato*, was put together in the cheapest way possible. Writer Niisan Takahashi had to invent a plotline that could incorporate the old Gamera footage mandated by Tokuma. Unable to rely on special effects gags and set pieces, this time, Takahashi would have to fashion more likeable characters to carry the movie. Whether or not he accomplished this is in the eye of the beholder, but Noriaki Yuasa at least had the good sense to cast beautiful women to inhabit those characters in an attempt to keep interest in however it was the film would turn out.

Try as they might (and try, they did), there was no way Yuasa and company was going to be able to turn in a decent Gamera adventure. The resultant film comes off exactly as it is: a cheap cash-grab. But it's not one by the filmmakers (they certainly weren't paid much to make the movie), but by a cynical producer only interested in exploiting a marketable name. A good movie could have been produced from this project if someone had done their job properly. Noriaki Yuasa did his job. Niisan Takahashi did his job. Shunsuke Kikuchi did his job (turning in probably his best score for the four Gamera films he worked on). Zenko Miyazaki did an amazing job editing the footage from the previous seven films together in a semi-cohesive unit. It was Yasuyoshi Tokuma who didn't do his job properly and allocate the money necessary to make a monster movie.

Tokuma might have claimed the new Gamera movie was being made by "New Daiei" and Daiei's company mark is slapped onto the film for old-times' sake, but there was no real Daiei ("new" or otherwise) and there was no real movie. After an almost non-stop string of popular, successful adventures, Gamera was forced to go out not with a bang, but with an optical flash whisper. But at the end of the day, the people who actually made it were not to blame.

And now that you know the story of its unfortunate birth, let's get into it...

CHAPTER TWO

UCHU KAIJU GAMERA

GAMERA SUPER MONSTER

COMMENTARY

Have you got your Blu-ray or DVD on hand? Is it loaded up and ready to go? No? Well, go get it, cause we're about to sit down and watch this sucker.

Got it now? Good. On the count of three, we'll begin.

One...
Two...
Three.

0:00:01
The movie jumps in feet first with lies and more lies. Daiei Motion Picture Company did not distribute this movie. Shochiku did. Gamera is not a space monster. And the movie was not produced by Daiei Motion Picture Company. It was produced—such that it was—by Tokuma Publishing.

0:00:11
Gamera, Super Monster was originally released in Japan on March 20th, 1980. Mid-March is the Spring Break season for kids in Japan and as such, was the time of Gamera. All of the films except for *Gamera*, *Gamera vs. Barugon*, *Gamera vs. Zigra*, *Gamera 2: Advent of Legion*, and *Gamera: Little Braves* were released around this time. In fact, *Super Monster* shares its release date with *Gamera vs. Viras.*

Super Monster was released on a double bill with the animated film, *Astro Boy: Earth Defense Corps*. This was the standard operating procedure for Gamera because all the movies to this point had been released on double bills. In—

1965: *Gamera* with *New Kurama Tengu: Gojozaka Duel*
1966: *Gamera vs. Barugon* with *Majin*
1967: *Gamera vs. Gaos* with *Little Fugitive*
1968: *Gamera vs. Viras* with *100 Ghost Stories*
1969: *Gamera vs. Guiron* with *Along With Ghosts*
1970: *Gamera vs. Jiger* with *Invisible Swordsman*
1971: *Gamera vs. Zigra* with a re-release of *Suzunosuke Akazodo: Third Bird Person*, a Daiei film from 1958.

0:01:48
This is not pre-production artwork. This entire sequence is made up of paintings from the art department specifically for this movie. Pre-production art is something directors and artists come up with as a design for something you're going to create more elaborately later on. These pieces of art were always going to be used as a device to set up the story they were telling from the get-go.

0:02:49
This is the introduction of the film's villain, Zanon. There seems to be some confusion as to what Zanon is in the west. "Zanon" is the name of the spaceship, the alien race, and the planet they hail from. The ship is ruled by the Zanon Captain, as he is billed in the opening titles. Japanese materials from the time have the name written as "Zanon-go" (in Japan, every type of ship or vehicle has the suffix "go"—which is not

meant to be pronounced—demarcating it as such). The soundtrack album for the film refers to the spaceship as "Space Monster Zanon Ship." Japanese Wikipedia refers to it as "Space Pirate Ship Zanon." Let's just say "Zanon" and be done with it.

There were two models of the Zanon spaceship made by the crew of this movie. One was very small made for long shots. The other was gigantic and required several crew members to haul it around.

0:03:06
This is the first of seven supposed "parody" scenes the theatrical program claims. This, of course, is "parodying" the original *Star Wars* (1977). Perhaps "parody" has a different meaning to the Japanese. Parody usually tends to have a mocking or humorous attitude about something. These parodies are more in line with the so-called parodies in the "Movie" movies, such as *Epic Movie*, *Disaster Movie*, or *Meet the Spartans* in which scenes and characters from other, better movies are trotted out and replayed for no real reason at all.

It would seem that *Gamera, Super Monster*'s Japanese form was meant to remind its audience of earlier, better entertainment. The title is meant to evoke nothing more than *Uchu Senken Yamato/Space Battleship Yamato*, which was extremely popular at the time. *Super Monster* was used as the English moniker in the west because "Space Battleship Yamato" wouldn't have any resonance outside Japan at the time.

The movie has three main titles. Its Japanese title is *Uchu Kaiju Gamera*/*Space Monster Gamera*. The international English title is *Super Monster*. Its U.S. release title is *Gamera, Super Monster*. There are no prints of the movie featuring the title *Super Monster Gamera* and it should not be referred to as such.

0:03:56
This is our introduction to pet store clerk Kilara, played by famed Japanese wrestling champ Mach Fumiake. Born March 3rd, 1959, her real name is Fumiake Watanabe and she was 20 years old when she shot the film (in late 1979) and had just turned 21 when the movie came out on March 20th. Fumiake wanted to be a singer from a young age and in 1972, appeared on the Japanese television show *Sutaa Tanjo! (Birth of a Star!*), a *Star Search*-style show taking its name from the Japanese release title of *A Star is Born*. Mach Fumiake made it to the final round but didn't win. At age 15, she decided to become a golfer because her uncle was also a golfer but her sister suggested she apply to a women's professional wrestling recruitment going on at the time. On March 19th, 1975—almost five years to the day of the release of this movie—she became the women's wrestling champion.

Mach Fumiake's height, attractiveness, and ability to sing changed the image of female wrestling and got people's attention, causing the sport to become very popular on Japanese TV. In 1976, she appeared in her first movie, Toei's *The Great Chase* starring Etsuko

"Sue" Shiomi. She appeared in a couple more movies before making *Super Monster* and subsequently, her biggest roles were as Akiyama in Juzo Itami's *A Taxing Woman* (1987) and *A Taxing Woman Returns* (1988). She also had a big presence on Japanese television throughout the 1980s. She has recently joined the cast of Kadokawa's *Nezura 1964* specifically because she's proud of starring in *Gamera, Super Monster.*

Fumiake moved to the United States in 1989 to attend Pepperdine University, studying health psychology and economics. She met her husband there and had two daughters in the early 1990s and remained in the States until around 2014 when she moved back to Japan and is still there currently, again working in performing arts. She also has a very fun, positive presence on Twitter where she will not hesitate to invoke the Kilara character.

0:04:09
Here, we are introduced to Mazda car dealer Marsha, played by Yaeko Kojima. Kojima is now known as the pop singer "Yaya." Kojima was likely also singing during the filming of this movie and first came to prominence doing so in 1982. She is still singing in Japan and has her own record label, which she started in 2014.

0:04:37
And here, were are introduced to school teacher Mitan, played by the innocent-looking Yoko Komatsu. Komatsu was specially skilled in Japanese dance and

jazz ballet. She had previously acted in the 1977 play *Good Luck Energy*. She appeared in quite a few television shows during the late '70s and was even cast by Noriaki Yuasa in *Ultraman 80* for the "Beautiful Challenger" episode, which would have been right after filming this movie.

0:05:00
While the film is obviously inspired by the 1978 *Superman: The Movie*, it seems to take it cue from the old 1950s *Superman* serials with George Reeves.

0:05:35
Folks, welcome to this absolutely nutastic movie. Thank you for joining me.

0:06:49
Hey, Kilara! Being pursued by an intergalactic warlord is *no* excuse to park like a jackhole.

0:07:45
Traveling to the earth in what appears to be glittery space sperm, we are introduced to the film's secondary antagonist, Giruge, played with zeal by Keiko Kudo. Kudo's real name is Keiko Sugiwara and she was born on March 27th, 1958. She can speak English and German fluently and was proficient in Japanese dance, aerobics, and swimming. Before *Super Monster*, Kudo had appeared as a nurse in an episode of the legendary Japanese TV show *G-Men '75* with the even more-legendary Tetsuro Tanba. After this film, she appeared in *Yokohama BJ Blues* in 1981, *Dangerous Criminal Case*

in 1987, *Twilight Mystery Nightmare Times 2* in 1991, and *Beautiful Girl Ladies!* in 1994. Following *Super Monster*, Kudo had a huge career on Japanese television. One such appearance was in episode 39 of *Ultraman Tiga*, "Dear Mr. Ultraman," in a small but prominently-featured role. She performed in the play *Flea in the Ear* and did a lot of commercial and radio work. She is still acting today.

0:08:24
Jeez, Giruge. Don't hate the player, hate the game, gurl.

0:08:47
Here, we are introduced to the audience surrogate, Keiichi Kinoshita played by child actor Koichi Maeda. He was 11 years old when cast in this film (in 1979). Maeda is still active in the entertainment industry both as an actor and as an agent, heading the Yaegeki Talent Office and is part of the Wakakusa theatre company. Though *Super Monster* is the only film he made, he had a successful career on Japanese television.

0:09:07
This whole sequence seems to be baffling to many western audiences. It turns out that this is all the second parody of the film, *Police Station in Front of Kameari Park*, a popular manga at the time. The kids are reading the manga itself in the scene. *Police Station in Front of Kameari Park* is about... well, a policeman who works at Kameari Park and his various

adventures in the vicinity. Why is this so confusing? Well, you kinda have to be a Japanese kid in 1980 to get it. Humor/references in Japanese films play with absolutely no context because they don't really care about appealing to outside audiences.

For example, in *Godzilla* (1984) when Godzilla topples the skyscraper onto the Super X and the building just slams against the ground without crumbling, this itself was a joke. In the early 80s as skyscrapers were becoming more common in Japan, there were contractors who boasted that their skyscrapers would not crumble during an earthquake. This, of course, left many Japanese remarking that "so the building will just fall over flat, then?" That scene is a reference to this, but how would you know that unless you were Japanese... in the early 1980s?

Keiichi's two pals here are billed as "Bad Boys" in the opening titles. I am finding it exceedingly difficult to refrain from making a *Cops* reference...

I hope you enjoyed this break in the action to read some *Police Station in Front of Kameari Park* and *Muscleman/Kinnikuman*.

0:10:03
This policeman is *not* Yuzo Hayakawa, Kawajiri from *Gamera vs. Barugon*, as is often erroneously reported (though it does look an awful lot like him). This is Koichi Takei, a popular Japanese comedian at the time and the artist who did the *Police Station in Front of*

Kameari Park manga. Takei was also featured prominently in the film's trailer (as was *Shonen Jump*, for that matter).

Koichi Takei is the man's real name, but he is known in Japan as "Bunraku Katsura (9th Generation)" [yes, "9th Generation" is part of his pseudonym]. The original Bunraku Katsura was a rakugoka (a form of Japanese professional storyteller) born in 1892!

Now that this madness has been thoroughly dissected and finally explained, let's all run out and buy a copy of *Shonen Jump*!

0:11:02
Holy hell does Keiichi's expression say it all...

0:11:08
The pet store Kilara works at is a real pet shop in Tokyo, Mon Toutou (as it says there in the window). They are given special thanks for cooperation in the shooting of the picture in the end titles.

0:11:46
Keiichi's turtle-talkin' shenanigans may seem a bit odd (as does Kilara's poor grasp of earth economics, for that matter), but he's still positively well-adjusted when compared to Toshio from the original *Gamera.* Hoo-boy...

0:12:42
The stock footage parade begins now, kicked off with the eruption of Mt. Fuji from the prologue of *Gamera vs. Gaos.*

0:14:15
Why is the guy center right *trying* to jump out of the helicopter if they're that high up??

0:14:31
According to the 40th Anniversary Gamera Lecture, an extra disc included with the DVD release of *Gamera: Little Braves*, this footage originally seen in *Gamera vs. Zigra* is of a type of F-104 fighter jet known as the "Last Manned Fighter." They look fairly impressive here, chiefly because those are real jets shot in cooperation with the military, but these sleek, (then) new jets don't mesh quite as well with the older 1967-type model jets when it cuts to the scene from *Gamera vs. Gaos.*

0:15:30
Here we have a reprise/cover of the main theme, *Love for Future*, which was sung over the opening titles by Mach Fumiake. The lyrics of the song were written by Hisashi Yama and the music was composed by Shunsuke Kikuchi. Fumiake also sang *As Long as You Are Alive* for the film, which only appeared on the B-side of the LP single release of *Love for Future*. The end credits of *Super Monster* are an adapted instrumental version of *As Long as You Are Alive.*

The tune of *Love for Future* would be utilized as Gamera's new theme music for this movie. Why the *Gamera March* wasn't utilized? I can only speculate it was because Hidemasa Nagata (Masaichi's son) wrote the lyrics to the song and he had nothing to do with this movie, so they couldn't use it. Again, just speculation.

0:16:00
If the fact that Keiichi has composed his own Gamera tribute song isn't enough to establish his super-monster super-fandom, the film cuts to a stack of Gamera magazines piled up on a table. Which, you know, #relatable.

Also, that middle image in the magazine (apparently made specifically for this film) is a picture of the new Gamera costume constructed for this film.

0:16:21
That is a maximum amount of mom face Keiichi's mother's got there.

Keiichi's mom is played by Toshie Takada, a fairly accomplished actress. She was born on March 3rd, 1935 (she shares a birthday with Mach Fumiake! There is an alarming connection between the month of March and this movie. For whatever it's worth, my birthday is in March too) and had appeared in over thirty movies by the time she made *Super Monster*! After this film, she would make several more theatrical features, but continued to have a gigantic career in

Japanese television series (like Keiko Kudo, she, too, was in *G-Men '75*) and Japanese made-for-TV movies. She is still alive today and her last appearance onscreen was in 2016's *Iyana Onna/Disgusting Woman.*

0:17:37
This whole bit with the turtle is not meant to imply some kind of new origin for Gamera. In fact, it is a backhanded swipe at the movie's audience! When *Gamera* first came out, there were Japanese children who thought their pet turtles were Gamera or would grow up to be Gamera. This whole thing with Keiichi and his turtle is a reference to that phenomena.

Western audiences often misinterpret these scenes to mean the Gamera in this movie is a new one not connected with the Gamera of the previous seven movies and that is incorrect. Tokuma's publicity for the film heavily implied that Gamera had been flying around in outer space since *Gamera vs. Zigra* and this was his long-awaited return to earth (did Gamera go stop the briefly-talked about Zigran invasion?!?). One of the taglines for the international poster even proclaims "Gamera returns from space!" You can't return from somewhere if you've never been there before in the first place.

This scene is a non-sequitur. No more, no less. More importantly though, this type of slice-of-life scene with a child is a showcase for the exact sort of sweetness that was always in Noriaki Yuasa's heart.

0:18:06
Here, we have the first wicked monster on the loose, Gaos/Gyaos. "Gaos" was Daiei's official English spelling of the character's name until they changed it to "Gyaos" in 1995 for *Gamera, Guardian of the Universe.* The international version of the movie features the super, "Supersonic Monster Gaos."

The monster's official stats and powers are:
Choonpa Kaiju Gyaosu/ Supersonic Monster Gaos
Height: 65 m (213 ft)
Weight: 25 tons
Wingspan: 172 m (564 ft)
Flight speed: Mach 3.5
Origin: Fossa Magna, Japanese archipelago
Weapons: Supersonic scalpel, Fire-extinguishing fluid

The name of the monster is properly said in English as "Gow-s" like Taos, New Mexico. "Guy-ohs" is incorrect.

In Japanese, the monster's name is said like "Gi-yow-s" with the "i" and the "y" sounds quickly together.

0:18:53
In the English dub, famed Hong Kong voice actor Ted Thomas does the narration here. His line is "The citizens of Nagoya were helpless. They found their weapons useless in their attempt to hold back the supersonic monster Gao—" It actually sounds like somebody tackled Thomas in the recording studio as he says the name "Gaos"!

0:19:07
Gamera, Super Monster functions both as a Gamera sampler platter for new fans and a (albeit, weird and lazy) love letter to the entire Showa series for series veterans.

0:20:36
If one looks carefully, they will see a dark skull on the sides of spaceship Zanon. Giruge has a similar skull on her belt when she first arrives in her uniform. A Television Land book about *Gamera, Super Monster* from the time of release shows the same skull to represent Zanon himself. It gives the invaders a jarring, almost demonic quality.

0:21:36
What kind of superheroines are these women?! Do *something*!

0:23:40
Either the call for Gamera to breathe fire and fight for those who can't or just *Love for Future* itself is inspiring the living hell out of Kilara. She's the best.

0:24:45
This scene seems rather random and doesn't make a whole lot of sense, but it is/was meant to serve an actual purpose. Having just learned of this "Gamera" from Keiichi, Kilara and her pals risk themselves to summon Gamera from wherever he is at this point. Unfortunately, the movie doesn't make this clear at all. Their attempt is cut off by Zanon's space lasers...

0:25:32
...but apparently, whatever it was the spacewomen did was successful because "the loud voice that crosses the galaxy" is back in Tokyo...

0:25:48
Here we have the first appearance of Super Monster Gamera. Let's look at those stats coming into the game:

Daikaiju Gamera/ Uchu Kaiju Gamera/ Cho Kaiju Gamera
Giant Monster Gamera/ Space Monster Gamera/ Super Monster Gamera
Origin: In the ice of the Arctic Ocean
Height: 60 m (200 ft)
Weight: 80 tons
Flight speed: Mach 3 when spinning

Gamera's looming appearance over Tokyo is the third "parody" of the film, this time of *Close Encounters of the Third Kind* (1977). I'm not sure I understand it either.

It is worth mentioning that this is the first time Gamera would have encountered skyscrapers. In Gamera's heyday, Japan didn't have buildings this tall, but in the late 1970s, skyscrapers began to be built in Japan. It could have been interesting if they'd thought to include a shot of Gamera having to sail around one.

0:26:06
Two flying Gamera marionettes were constructed for the film. The main one is the one we're seeing now. Other than shooting jet flames, all it can do is open and close its mouth. This was a result of the control mechanism being damaged and with no time/money to repair it, it became a matter of the mouth would open and close indefinitely or just stay closed. No in-betweens. This marionette is about the size of a tiger and required two grips to carry it around. A second, marionette (that could not open its mouth) with a length of about three feet was utilized for long shots.

0:26:32
Keiichi absolutely losing his mind as Gamera flies overhead cements him as the most relatable character in the movie.

0:26:51
Admittedly, it is hard to remember the warnings of stranger danger when the 200-foot flying turtle of your dreams has just sailed overhead. I can't blame him though; I like talking about Gamera to pretty girls who'll listen too.

0:27:13
In the English dub, most of the time, they mispronounce Gamera's name. In Europe (where *War of the Monsters* and *Return of the Giant Monsters* were dubbed—Rome, to be exact), they say it as "Guh-mare-uh." However, Daiei's official English pronunciation of Gamera (like "camera") would be

utilized for *Gammera, the Invincible* and AIP's dubs starting with *Destroy All Planets*. Daiei's international dubs would also use the "Gam-er-uh" pronunciation. However, with no Daiei around to tell the dubbers how to properly say it, the team in Hong Kong were left to their own devices. It is worth noting, though, that several times throughout the international dub, they do say his name as "Gam-er-uh," just not often.

In Japanese, Gamera's name is said as "Gah-may-rah."

0:28:01
It doesn't matter what movie it's in; this shot of Gamera spinning into the battle over the wrecked Nagoya set is beautiful.

0:29:03
Yuasa has said that they had to choose carefully when to have Gaos fire his "supersonic scalpel" ray. Every blast cost nearly $1,000 to have optically created out of house (Daiei did not have an optical printer like Eiji Tsuburaya did over at Toho).

0:30:18
So nobody at this Japanese elementary school noticed Giruge just loitering out front???

0:30:38
Hanging around elementary schools... harassing little kids... talking smack about Gamera. We... we had probably keep our eye on Giruge, if you know what I mean (and I think you do).

0:31:22
I love those "withdraw into his shell" Gamera puppets the Showa films used. The Heisei trilogy was sorely lacking them.

0:31:35
For the record, this is not a puppet. That's Teruo Aragaki in the Gamera suit constructed for *Gamera vs. Gaos*, pushing himself off the ground with his forearms.

0:31:50
While that was the Gaos suit in the background lifting into the air, this right here is a pair of gloves made to look like Gaos' feet that a crewman is using to grab Gamera's shell.

0:32:16
I've seen this shot in Daieiscope. I've seen this shot in standard widescreen. I've seen this shot cropped into fullscreen. I've seen it in standard and high definition and for the life of me, I can't really tell what actually happens in the shot. I'm told it's supposed to be Gamera knocking Gaos' feet out from under him with his tail. I mean, I guess... ?

0:33:06
It seems surprising to me that these shots were even included here. While *Gamera vs. Gaos* boasts decent special effects, these shots of a Gamera toy/model dragging Gaos up the side of the volcano were inadequate back in 1967, let alone 1980.

0:33:46
The new scenes of this movie were shot by Akira Kitazaki...

0:33:48
Kitazaki, you magnificent bastard. That is some A-1 framing.

0:34:15
Western audiences often misinterpret scenes like this where Keiichi's mother has no interest in monster shenanigans or that nothing about Gamera's fighting is in the newspapers to mean that the action of this film is just a dream or it's all in Keiichi's mind. That is not the correct thought to have. It stems from a misguided overthinking of the matter. This is a movie made for 10-year-olds, not late 20-somethings trying to justify what they're watching with mental gymnastics.

If we absolutely *have* to think like this, it could be construed that monsters have become passé in Japan by this point. Maybe today, a mother has no interest in following the exploits of Billie Eilish. That does not mean Eilish doesn't exist. And Gamera fought Gaos out in the country in the middle of the night. Probably nobody even saw it and certainly no reporters were there to write about it. But again: mental gymnastics. In short, just roll with it. Unless you're a child, this movie wasn't made for you, so maybe ease up on it.

0:35:07
This shot of Giruge teleporting in the middle of a crowd (which they somehow do not notice) is surprisingly well done in comparison to other shots in the movie utilizing this trick. The other people walking around seem reasonably placed to match their movements in the other shot before Giruge is inserted into the scene.

0:35:36
<u>HAMBURGERLUNCH</u>!

I have to admit that I would probably sell the earth out to Giruge. Especially if she took me out for hamburgerlunch.

0:37:07
I imagine this is probably what a Doors music video would've looked like.

0:37:27
Apparently, some crew member's job was to toss kids around all day. Good work if you can get it.

0:37:37
Keiichi informally refers to both Kilara and Giruge as "one'-san" (pronounced "oh-nay-san"), which means "older sister" or "sis." This will come into shape later in the movie as it's revealed Keiichi is an only child and wishes to have a sister. Since Keiichi's mom and his barely-mentioned father can't be bothered to get

busy, a surrogate sister will do for him. Really what Keiichi is probably looking for is a role model.

0:38:03
This repurposing of Zigra's starship's fin as Zigra himself is meant to evoke *Jaws* (1975), the fourth parody of the film.

0:38:32
It is worth pointing out that if an old school "monster kid" Gamera fan were watching these movies in order they came out in the United States, *Super Monster* would have been the first time they would have seen any footage from *Gamera vs. Zigra*. Because Daiei was bankrupt when that film was released (and had to be released in Japan by Dainichi Films), AIP was unable to get the rights to the movie when it was new. As a result, *Zigra* was never released in the United States until 1987 when Sandy Frank got the rights to five Gamera films and put them on VHS.

0:38:58
Shinkai Kaiju Jigura/ Deep Sea Monster Zigra
Origin: Star System No. 105, 4th Planet Zigra
Height: 80 m (262 ft) [this is presumably the standing land version]
Weight: 75 tons
Weapons: Three-Color Light Beam

0:39:51
While it's obvious these scenes are shot on "dry" sets, they look believably underwater thanks to some trick

photography. Lights dazzling overhead look like sunlight shining through and occasionally an actual water tank was placed in front of the camera to shoot through real water for bubbles and other aquatic atmosphere.

0:40:11
While it's not as noticeable here in *Super Monster*, in *Gamera vs. Zigra*, it's interesting to note that it's very visible that the slices Zigra inflicts onto Gamera form the Japanese character "ki," which means "strength."

0:40:30
So were Keiichi and Giruge just standing there looking at the water this whole time? Or what did they talk about while they were waiting for Gamera to surface? Were there more hamburgers about?

0:40:38
This is a halfway decent attempt to marry the stock footage with the new footage, having Keiichi knocked off his feet by Zigra hitting the ground. It could've played a little better if Giruge had wobbled around as well, but perhaps being an alien, she just has better footing.

0:40:40
Gamera vs. Zigra is the only movie where we for sure do not know who played Gamera. In *Gamera*, he was played predominately by Kazuo Yagi (as well as the entire Daiei effects team, but most of the time, it was Yagi). In *Gamera vs. Barugon* through *Gamera vs. Viras*,

he was played by Teruo Aragaki. In *Gamera vs. Guiron* and *Gamera vs. Jiger*, he was played by Umenosuke Izumi. There is really no reason to believe Izumi did not play Gamera in *Zigra* as well (considering they recycled the suit from *Jiger*, which was built for him), but there is nothing to substantiate it. Such information could have possibly been destroyed in the Daiei riot.

Speaking of, in his commentary for *Gamera vs. Barugon*, August Ragone postulates that Barugon was played by Umenosuke Izumi. Considering he would play Gamera after Teruo Aragaki left, it seems reasonable to assume that if so, Izumi also played Gaos and Viras similar to how Kenpachiro Satsuma began his suitmation career as Hedorah and Gigan in the 70s before graduating to Godzilla for the Heisei series. This, however, is pure conjecture on my part.

0:41:16
Look carefully and you'll see Zigra's head start to fall apart when it hits the ground. So instead of rubber like usual, Zigra's head was constructed from metal apparently. It's at least a little reasonable that such footage make it into the final cut of *Gamera vs. Zigra*, but to repeat it here is foolhardy at best, unobservant at worst.

0:41:21
In *Gamera vs. Zigra*, when Gamera does this, he played the tune of the *Gamera March*. Since the March isn't

utilized for this movie, Shunsuke Kikuchi had to compose new musical notes for Zigra's fins to play.

0:41:50
This is the best subgenre in the universe. And I think Gamera just Scorpion'd Zigra...

0:42:15
Despite the fact in the Japanese dialogue and the Japanese opening credits, she is explicitly identified as "Giruge," the international dub seems to rename her "Giloke." Again, with no Daiei extant, there was no one to tell the international dubbers what the names were and how to say them properly. When I saw the movie as a child, I thought they were calling her "Yellowkey."

0:44:27
Look carefully and you'll notice Keiichi's hair is slightly different now, betraying that this scene was shot at a different time than the others surrounding it. Or maybe Kilara let Keiichi comb it while Giruge was cursing her luck. Either way, it's poor continuity.

0:45:05
If the Zanon Captain is so dissatisfied with Giruge's performance, why doesn't he just bring his sorry conquistador ass down and do it himself? He's got a big-ass spaceship to sail around in. What's he afraid of down here on earth? And why does Giruge just let him talk to her this way?

0:47:22
Uchu Kaiju Bairasu/ Suichu Kaiju Bairasu
Outer Space Monster Viras/ Underwater Monster Viras
Origin: Space
Height: 96 m (315 ft)
Weight: 120 tons
Weapons: 6 free-moving arms, 3-dividing head

Even though both the dubs for this movie and *Destroy All Planets* feature the monster's name being pronounced "Vee-russ," it should be properly said just like "virus." The character's Japanese name is spelled "Bairasu," which is pronounced "bye-russ." If "Vee-russ" were meant to be the monster's name, the Japanese would spell it "Birasu" ["bee-russ"]. In Japanese, there are no v's, so those words have to be transliterated to a b sound. Daiei's international dub for *Gamera vs. Guiron* properly pronounces the name as "virus."

Viras' general nickname is uchu kaiju/space monster, but since they were already calling Gamera "uchu kaiju" for this movie, Viras' nickname was changed to "underwater monster."

0:47:41
For the record again, Viras is a suit here, not a puppet. Ryosaku Takayama was the man who designed the suits for these Gamera opponents and Viras was his favorite of the bunch. Takayama also designed the original Godzilla suit way back in 1954.

0:48:27
Doesn't Viras' face look a lot like the alien Balok puppet from the original *Star Trek* series?

0:48:43
Super Monster fixes an editorial mistake here that was left in *Gamera vs. Viras*. In *Viras*, the Gamera model floats back to the top of the water. This movie properly cuts away while the model is still submerged.

0:49:12
While we can't really see to substantiate it, I believe Gamera is supposed to be literally jet skiing in this sequence, using his rear jets to propel him across the water.

0:49:31
When this happened in *Gamera vs. Viras*, it caused the children in the audience to scream with fright.

0:49:49
This insert here of Gamera's jets blasting on is a brand new shot.

0:50:00
Viras didn't really think this through, did he?

0:50:47
I really don't like how Giruge's immediate reaction to being scolded by the Zanon Captain is to drop to her knees...

0:52:16
While this scene of Gamera inexplicably encountering Space Battleship Yamato in its original animated form is meant to be a dream Keiichi is having, it's very possible this is where Gamera is at the current moment. *Gamera vs. Viras* had already established that Gamera does patrol the area around the earth for possible threats.

0:52:21
This is music not composed by Shunsuke Kikuchi, but is the actual, factual Space Battleship Yamato theme song, composed by Hiroshi Miyagawa.

As Gamera eyeballs the Yamato and it beats feet away, he doesn't seem especially hostile toward it.

0:54:40
Why are there just a bunch of tires piled up on the top of this parking garage?

0:54:56
These composite shots of the spacewomen in their pet carrier case are surprisingly well-done. The glass even warps a little bit at the top of the case there.

0:55:13
Zanon's gone too far this time. You don't mess with someone's wheels!

0:56:52
Giruge's skulking around the pet shop here because she's got a court order to stay 500 light years away from the school. That's what you get for trash talking Gamera to little kids.

0:57:23
While she may be out to destroy the country, you have to admit Giruge is getting a pretty nice tour of Japan out of it.

0:57:34
Should we be led to believe Zanon just dumped poor Jiger out onto an unsuspecting Osaka?

Daimaju Jaiga/ Giant Demon Beast Jiger
Origin: Wester Island, near equator
Length: 80 m (262 ft)
Weight: 200 tons
Weapons: Magnetism Ray, Solidified Saliva Missiles, Egg-Laying Tube

The international version of the movie strangely uses the super "Giant Space Monster Jiger." The Japanese super there properly says "Daimaju Jaiga/Giant Demon Beast Jiger."

0:57:58
Gamera vs. Jiger looks a little healthier than the past two Gamera films thanks to an influx of money from Expo '70. However, the tradeoff was that Yuasa wasn't allowed to have the monsters destroy any of

the Expo buildings. Was Expo '70 not familiar with how Japanese monster movies work??

0:58:43
As Gamera readies himself to absolutely hand Jiger's ass to her for causing trouble in Osaka, it is worth noting something about Gamera that a lot of fans fail to pick up on when they talk about what would happen if Gamera and Godzilla ever fought. Though unlikely, an enemy monster can survive a battle with Godzilla. If they flee, he will generally let them go. However, Gamera will straight up murder his enemies in front of children. He drowns Barugon, he drags Gaos into an active volcano, he freezes Viras then shatters him into pieces, he shoves a statue through Jiger's forehead, and roasts Zigra alive [I am still not exactly sure what happened to Guiron. It's just so poorly shot and edited!].

It can't be seen well here in *Super Monster* due to the quicker editing, but if you look carefully in *Gamera vs. Gaos*, when Gamera bites Gaos' foot in Nagoya Bay, the first thing he does is attempt to drag Gaos underwater to drown him too! Gamera is hardcore. So maybe take that into account before you proclaim that Godzilla would absolutely decimate Gamera.

Also, while artists tend to draw Godzilla towering over Gamera, Gamera is usually the taller monster. In the Showa series, Gamera was 60 meters tall and in the Heisei series, 80 meters tall (for all three films/forms). The only standard Godzillas taller than

Gamera are the later Heisei and *Final Wars* incarnations, both of whom were 100 meters tall.

0:59:25
I'm almost certain this flying Gamera prop is a repurposed model from *Gamera vs. Barugon*. The angry-looking eyes look very much like the suit's eyes from that particular film.

1:00:18
Using this shot of Jiger trying to use her suction feet to draw in Gamera re-contextualized as Jiger in her death throes is especially clever and inventive.

1:00:26
So did Giruge just spend the night there in the ruins of Osaka?

1:00:32
I've had about enough of this Zanon guy's crap. Oh, now you're gonna kill her? Yeah, big, tough intergalactic warlord has to threaten women. Come on, Zanon. Why don't you get your ass down here and we'll settle this thing like men?

Wait, what's happening?

1:01:03
If you've seen a few of these Gamera films, you'll notice that Gamera never actually lands. He either crashes into something or just falls out of the air. This here, however, is one of his savvier "landings."

1:01:12
Giruge's windswept hair looks gooooooooood...

1:01:19
New shot of Gamera here of the controller blasted onto his neck. Yuasa should be given credit for not somehow reusing the extremely similar footage of this same thing happening in *Gamera vs. Viras* instead.

1:01:40
Since this is the third time Gamera's destroyed the Kurobe Dam (previously in *Gamera vs. Barugon* and *Gamera vs. Viras**), you'd think they would just stop rebuilding the damn thing.

*technically, Gamera is forced to destroy the fictional "Oku-Musashi Dam" in *Viras*, but still...

1:02:12
I don't believe Gamera is supposed to be exhaling flames as an attack here. I mean, maybe he is in the context of *Super Monster*, but in *Gamera vs. Barugon*, I think he's supposed to be eating the flames from the destruction he's caused at Kurobe Dam.

1:02:33
At the very least, you'd think they could try to reinforce the dam to withhold Gamera's ramming if they must keep rebuilding it.

1:03:03
This is also clever repurposing of footage from *Gamera vs. Jiger*, making Gamera's painful staggering to the seaside after being poisoned by Jiger's egg seem like he's destroying the city here.

1:03:16
Here we have some of the only footage in the film of the new suit made for the film. There was an entire new Gamera costume constructed for the film. Footage of the suit being built can be found in part two of the *Gamera Special* on the Arrow Blu-ray set. At any rate, the suit wasn't built just for feet to walk across the screen. There were meant to be actual new scenes of Gamera filmed for the movie. There exists at least one still filming the Gamera suit in a small miniature set. If the end titles are to be believed, as "monster operator" Gamera was portrayed by Toru Kawai, who had previously played Godzilla in *Zone Fighter* (1973) and *Terror of Mechagodzilla* (1975), as well as the monstrous Tyrannosaurus Rex in *The Last Dinosaur* (1977). He holds the rare distinction of being the only actor to have played both Godzilla and Gamera.

The special effects for this film were shot using the Vistavision Totsu ECG system, which had previously been used extensively for Toei's *Message from Space* (1978). It used videotape rather than celluloid film, but as many elements as were wanted could be put into the shot and was much cheaper to use. Using optical effects on film, a duplicate print has to be struck of each element needed for the shot, causing a degradation of the image (this is why the Japanese opening credits look the peculiar way they do—the elements were mastered from videotape). Whenever everything is put together satisfactorily, then that footage is transferred to 35mm film.

The Vistavision Totsu ECG system was an unperfected process and something went wrong with the footage, making the new scenes featuring the Gamera suit unusable. Without proper funds to make the movie in the first place, Yuasa was unable to reshoot the footage. Consequently, only the shot of Gamera's feet and a later shot of Gamera flying made it into the final film (a similar thing occurred shooting *Message from Space*. An entire effects sequence had to be dropped from the end of the movie because of a Vistavision mishap). They also had an initial problem they had to get around in that the Vistavision process was making Gamera's jet flames too bright.

The Gamera suit constructed for this film wound up being used far more extensively for a Kalgon snack food campaign in 1989! Two of these ads can be viewed on YouTube.

1:03:28
Oooh! Somebody better get Godzilla some salve for that burn!

The roadshow poster here is for a fake film titled *Saraba, Dojira*. "Dojira" [dough-jee-lah] could be translated as "Dogzilla." The title in English is *Farewell, Dojira/Dogzilla.* It wasn't really intended as a jab at Godzilla as most westerners seem to think. It was more a commentary from Noriaki Yuasa that there hadn't been any Godzilla movies for years now. This was him sort of saying, "Hey, where's Godzilla?" Unlike Toho with Gamera, Yuasa never saw Godzilla as their rival; he saw Godzilla as their teacher.

At any rate, the fifth "parody" is, of course, Godzilla.

1:03:35
The TV announcer here is real-life news personality Yasuhiro Saito of Nippon Broadcasting.

1:03:46
While Keiichi and Kilara legitimately seem invested in what they're watching, Marsha and Mitan look like they're just spacing out until Channel 12's Nightly News announces the Powerball numbers.

1:03:54
The footage from the first Gamera movie, *Giant Monster Gamera*, has been tinted a peach/slight red color to make us think it's in color as if lit by the flames. This trick had previously been employed for footage from the first movie in *Gamera vs. Viras.* However, in remastered prints, it's fully in black and white because the color elements have been lost. But in Daiei's old 90s laserdisc of the 90-minute cut of the film, the *Gamera* footage in *Viras* looks just like this.

1:04:45
I think this is the first time in the movie's new footage that we see the smaller, three-foot-long flying Gamera marionette. The one that couldn't open its mouth.

1:04:58
Apparently, nobody told the artist who did this work that Gamera doesn't fly through the air like Superman. Likely, there was no money for another go.

1:05:27
The spacewomen from the peaceful star M88 may be the least effective heroines in history. Kilara claims they are not "allowed" to have any weapons to fight with. Allowed by whom? It's been established that Zanon destroyed M88 and Kilara, Marsha, and Mitan are the last inhabitants of the world extant. There's nobody around to stop them from doing whatever they need to for the sake of peace. Old habits die hard, I guess.

1:06:29
Spaceship Zanon looks like it needs a V-8...

1:06:47
This appears to be new footage of the Gamera suit rather than footage of the flying marionette. Look closely and you'll see the hand is shaped differently than the marionette's and can move while the marionette's cannot.

There appear to be five different elements making up

this shot. 1.) the cityscape below, 2.) Gamera's head, 3.) Gamera's shell, 4.) Gamera's hand, and 5.) Kilara flying onto Gamera.

1:06:50
Certainly, this mock-up of Gamera's shell and neck that Kilara lands on are brand new and built specifically for this movie.

1:07:06
Why was there not a *Captain Marvel* made in the early 80s starring Mach Fumiake??

1:07:26
Strangely enough, Gamera doesn't seem to be flying any differently under his own will as he was under Zanon's control. Is Gamera even aware that he was under alien control? Did he care?

1:08:00
Why are these space aliens so chicly dressed??

1:08:09
Was Giruge packing a miniature maser gun in her purse this whole time??? And if so, why wasn't she using that bad boy?

1:08:43
Everybody hush up a minute. Girl fight!

1:08:53
If there was ever any doubt as to whether or not I'd sell out the earth to Giruge, it's completely gone now. Dem getaway sticks, yo... #TeamGiruge

1:09:16
A lot has been said about Mach Fumiake's Amazonian appearance, but do keep in mind Keiko Kudo is only 5'3 and weighs roughly 105 pounds. So, Fumiake's not actually as big as she appears here.

1:09:36
Yeesh. Giruge may be the unluckiest alien invader in the history of tokusatsu. Certainly, she's one of the most inept. There has to be *some* reason the Zanon Captain made her the vanguard of his invasion, right?

Right... ?

1:10:40
At the risk of thinking too much about it (again, movie made for 10-year-olds), it would seem that Giruge has never been shown kindness or affection in her life and doesn't know how to deal with it—YIKES! Well, this took a hard left turn!

1:11:09
Daiakuju Giron/ Giant Evil Beast Guiron
Origin: 10th planet Tera
Length: 85 m (279 ft)
Weight: 110 tons
Weapons: Sharp head, shuriken firing

For some reason, in the *Attack of the Monsters* dub, Guiron's name is pronounced "Gweer-on." In Daiei's international dub, they say Guiron's name properly as "Gyour-on." For what it's worth, his Japanese name is pronounced "Gi-ron."

1:11:20
The American version of the movie retains the original Japanese monster introduction supers (with no translation provided). This is likely because the movie was going to be sent direct to television and the English supers in the international version stretched entirely across the screen whereas the Japanese supers were centralized in the middle of the frame. To use the English supers, either the words on either edge would be cut off or the movie would randomly stretch for those shots. The American version does utilize the international version's opening and ending credits (with an altered title card, though).

1:11:37
These are marionettes/puppets in this shot, not actors in monster suits.

1:11:46
Guiron was supposed to be a completely bipedal monster, but because the head was so heavy for the suit actor the wear, Yuasa decided to make him a predominately quadruped monster so the actor could move better.

1:11:53
New Gamera shot insert!

1:12:08
These gymnastic shenanigans were included in *Gamera vs. Guiron* because the Olympics in Mexico City had just happened in summer 1968. Yuasa thought the kids would love it. The trailer even boasted "Space is the arena for the Monster Olympics!"

1:12:26
Gamera got 10s from everybody except that stuck-up judge from Rolisica who won't give anybody higher than an 8.

1:12:35
New Gamera shot insert!

1:12:40
"Looks like you took a sharp turn into Knife City, pal!"

1:13:24
This shot here was a reference to Daiei's popular Zatoichi series and Gamera is using the icicle like the blind swordsman's sword-cane he carried with him.

1:13:34
Again, *Super Monster* fixes an editing error in the original movie. In *Gamera vs. Guiron*, the take of Gamera standing there lasts too long and it plays like he just randomly falls into the Teran lake. Here, the

footage has been fixed to properly look like Gamera jerks himself back too far and it made him fall backwards.

1:14:10
They totally hoped you wouldn't notice there's no reason in the context of this movie for that rocket to fire. In *Gamera vs. Guiron*, Akio shoots it off semi-accidentally.

1:14:18
Uh, kids... don't play with missiles.

1:14:33
I have been watching this (as *Gamera vs. Guiron*) since, like, 1991 and for the life of me, I still can't tell what is supposed to have happened to Guiron here. It looks like maybe his head was blown off... but then, as he expires, Guiron's head is still neatly attached to his body. See the arms there?

1:14:40
It's entirely likely this shot of Gamera throwing his arms into the air was repeated here due to the phenomenal success of *Rocky* and *Rocky II* by the time this film had been made. They probably wanted you to think Gamera was striking the Rocky pose.

1:14:52
Uh, Gamera... perhaps you should check for any other monsters Zanon might be holding there before you go back to earth? Gamera? Er, Gamera... ?

1:15:02
Here, we get a cameo from the eponymous *Galaxy Express 999* [properly said as "Galaxy Express Three Nine"]. While the encounter with Space Battleship Yamato was just a dream Keiichi was having, this could logically be happening. Galaxy Express 999 can travel across dimensions similar to the Doctor [Who]'s Tardis, so it is plausible that Three-Nine briefly came into Gamera's universe and then left. Gamera does seem fairly tolerant about spying it, though.

1:15:50
Again, movie made for 10-year-olds. Let's everybody calm down.

1:16:30
Keiichi's a good egg.

1:17:01
Reito Kaiju Barugon/ Chilling Monster Barugon
Origin: Rainbow Valley, New Guinea
Length: 80 m (262 ft)
Weight: 70 tons
Weapons: Chilling Liquid, Rainbow-Colored Murder Rays

1:17:39
At the time of this film's release, there was a character who appeared at live attraction shows who does not appear in the movie. They were similar to Kamen Rider and was said to come from the same planet as the spacewomen (Peace Planet M88 or "the Peaceful

Star M88" in the dub). The figure wore a helmet and full-body tights so they could be portrayed by a man or a woman, depending on who was available at the venue. At these same attraction shows, both Mach Fumiake in full Kilara regalia and the new Gamera costume were on hand to promote the film.

1:19:14
Honestly, I'll be damned if I know how they made this jet model fall apart, but it works great.

1:19:27
Wakka-jaw, wakka-jaw, wakka-jaw, wakka-jaw...

1:19:58
Barugon nuking a missile array with a weaponized rainbow is Gamera's cue to light his trifflin' ass up!

1:20:16
I suppose it's poetic that Gamera's last opponent of the film is his first, but it seems awfully anticlimactic considering Barugon isn't that threatening an enemy compared to previous monsters. His main danger was in freezing Gamera, which has been eschewed in this re-edit of the two fights.

1:20:44
I'm not sure but I think we just teleported from Osaka Castle to Lake Biwa??

1:20:50
If you look very carefully, even though the long shot of Barugon jumping/sailing at Gamera was removed from this movie, at least one frame of that shot wound up making it into the assembly here.

1:21:10
For no discernible reason, Barugon suddenly starts belting out Yongary's voice from *Yongary, Monster from the Deep* (1967)! This could very well be a joke by Yuasa. At the very end of *Yongary*, as the monster is dying and falling through some bridges, he starts snorting out Barugon's voice!

1:21:40
I think it's worth mentioning that this fight works a lot better here scored with actual music than it does in its own movie. The fights in *Gamera vs. Barugon* bizarrely go unscored for most of the bouts, with just sound effects and monster roars on the soundtrack. Let's not make any pretenses of "Oh, that's more realistic, though." I'm not gonna listen to any "realism" talk revolving around a rainbow-shooting chameleon and a jet-powered, flying turtle.

1:22:37
Did we hit another wrinkle in time?

1:23:04
Marsha, Mitan, and Keiichi seem thrilled to see Barugon drowning to death. Those shameless

gorehounds. One of them will probably suggest they watch *The Beyond* next. My money's on Mitan...

1:23:08
Here's a nice touch, either by writer Niisan Takahashi or improvised by Keiko Kudo. Look carefully in the back at Giruge. Even though she seems to be on the good side now, she still snaps her fingers with disappointment as Gamera spins away in victory. Again, old habits die hard.

1:23:33
Again, another interesting character moment, this time by the rest of the cast. I can't help but notice as they charge off, they have no qualms about leaving Giruge's crippled ass behind. In the next scene, she can be seen hobbling up behind them.

1:24:31
I don't know about the rest of you, but I think Giruge is mad sexier in her earthling "disguise" than in her militant Zanon uniform. Perhaps that's the point?

1:24:43
Whoa! Giruge took that orbital positronic blast like a *boss*! I mean, sure, she crumpled to the ground and died a minute or so later, but she legit stood there, let them shoot her with an interplanetary laser blast to her chest and stood on her feet through 99% of it. That’s baller as hell, y'all. Like Dwayne Johnson-level *Baller*[*s*]. Again, #TeamGiruge

It's like something Gamera would do... Say, why is he repeatedly flying around in a furious tizzy... ?

1:25:54
Here, there are two "parodies" thrown together for the price of one. Number six is Keiichi calling for Gamera to come back, meant to evoke the classic western *Shane* (1953). When the scene cuts to outer space, number seven apes the final moments of the most recent Space Battleship Yamato movie, *Farewell Space Battleship Yamato: Warriors of Love* (1978). While the ending of that film is far superior artistically to the one here, it is viscerally much less satisfying. It closes with a battered Yamato sailing off into the distance to meet the wicked Gamilas' ship and then you see a massive explosion (implying the two ships collided) and the end titles run. In fact, *Gamera, Super Monster*'s storyline seems suspiciously close to that of *Farewell Space Battleship Yamato.*

1:26:21
This is what the showdown of *The Good, The Bad, and The Ugly* would have been like had Sergio Leone not known what the hell he was doing.

1:26:55
Real talk, though: this is what bravery looks like.

1:27:08
"Ul-tra-man..."

1:27:16
Oh, I can't wait to see Gamera fly by the Zanon model and blast it with fake fire of some kind while he dodges animated laser beams...

1:27:23
WHAT?!?

1:27:32
Say what you want but Koichi Maeda is selling this for all it's worth.

1:27:43
Noriaki Yuasa has mentioned that originally Gamera lived at the end of this movie; that Niisan Takahashi's script ended the same way every other Gamera movie ended: with Gamera flying off in the distance and everyone relieved. However, he saw how poorly the movie was going and realized Gamera could never come back from it, so he decided to kill him off. Perhaps this was also a stab at Tokuma, preventing them from further exploiting Gamera. "It was a very strange fate for my son," Yuasa said.

However, on Arrow's release for this film, in their photo gallery, there is an image of Kilara, Marsha, Mitan, and Keiichi all wearing coats, smiling, and waving to something ahead of them. This heavily implies that the Gamera lives happy ending was shot after all. In the scene found in the movie, only Keiichi is wearing a coat. It also goes a long way to explain the severe mood whiplash of the film where everyone's bummed out that Gamera died then suddenly happy to sail around Tokyo. Kilara, especially, seems a little too blaze` about Gamera being gone in the final cut of the movie.

Is it possible that Gamera was always going to ram himself into the Zanon ship and the explosion would be a fake-out making everyone think Gamera died but then he is revealed to be flying off in the distance? With both Yuasa and Takahashi gone now, we may never know.

1:29:05
This is the eighth and last (*hmm...*) of the supposed parodies of the film, this time of the 1978 *Superman*, mirroring Superman and Lois Lane's flight over Metropolis.

1:29:29
The trailer for *Gamera, Super Monster* is hysterical and over-hypes the film like you would not believe. The narration tries to trick its juvenile audience with deception, claiming *Super Monster* is a "monumental movie" and that the end showdown between Gamera and Zanon is "exciting" and "thrilling." A later trailer or TV spot (or something) hyped the movie up with lines like "Great monster movie masterpiece! Gamera has returned!" and "Historical fun! Take this chance— don't let it go!" Can you believe the balls on the Tokuma publicity department? Then again, they thought this film would work, so...

The international English trailer with voiceover narration by Ted Thomas is every bit its bizarre equal. Forgetting the fact that he mispronounces Mach Fumiake's name—the likes of which haven't been heard since "Adele Dazeem"—Thomas claims *Super Monster* is "a space movie on a gigantic scale" and "*Super Monster* is the most riveting film in the history of motion pictures!" Look, I will defend this movie till my dying breath, but those are some straight-up, flat-out, boldfaced **LIES**. I hope Thomas got paid well, at least. The international trailer also can't seem to make up its mind what the title is. It alternates between both "Super Monster" and "Gamera - The Supermonster" [sic], sometimes within seconds of each other!

1:30:24
On March 25th, 1995, just weeks after *Gamera, Guardian of the Universe* opened, a videogame titled *Gamera: The Time Adventure* was released for an obscure console only available in Japan called the Playdia by Bandai. It was more or less *Gamera, Super Monster: The Game*. The Zanon aliens invade the earth and Gamera appears. The player takes the role of something called "the Time Police" who do not trust Gamera for some reason. So, they have to travel through the past Showa Gamera films (and sometimes help Gamera defeat his opponents) and collect things called "time records." If you transverse the game and collect all the time records, you as the player help Gamera fight the Zanon spaceship and Gamera gets to live this time. While the game was heavily steeped in the Showa series, it was bridged slightly with the new film by

featuring Ayako Fujitani—Asagi Kusanagi from *Guardian of the Universe*—as... Ayako the Navigator. And honestly, couldn't *Super Monster* have benefited from Fujitani's presence? And money? And new monster footage? And a producer that gave a damn about the movie being good?

1:31:23
The German dub for the movie inserts actual new dialogue here with Kilara and Keiichi while the original Japanese dialogue and the English dub remains silent. I do not speak German well enough to relay what's being said (Keiichi's response to whatever Kilara is saying is "ja/yes").

If you managed to make it this far, I hope you learned something about this most misunderstood of the Gamera films and perhaps even gained a new appreciation for it. Thank you for coming to my TED Talk.

Until next time, this is Constantine Furman reminding you that referring to every child regardless of race or gender in a monster movie as "Kenny" is racist as hell. It doesn't make you hip or above it all; it just makes you seem peer-pressured, imperceptive, and mean.

CHAPTER THREE

LEGACY

Uchu Kaiju Gamera opened to disastrous results on March 20th, 1980. It performed pretty much the way Noriaki Yuasa expected it would. Tokuma didn't get the quick cash they'd hoped for. Daiei was still dead. But worst of all, Gamera was over.

Ever since its release, *Super Monster* garnered a reputation of being the worst of the worst. I've seen the worst and I wish *Super Monster* was as bad as it got (*Super Monster* isn't even the worst tokusatsu movie ever made. Have you seen *Gunhed*?). Noriaki Yuasa didn't like the movie and rarely talked about it (though, obviously, he was rarely asked about it). The movie is a product of its time and circumstances and while it may not be especially good, it's not awful either. What is the difference between watching *Super Monster* and watching *Gamera vs. Barugon* for the tenth time? You've already seen the latter movie. *Super Monster* just had it in different packaging.

At any rate, Daiei did manage to make their way into filmmaking again (with Yasuyoshi Tokuma now its head rather than Masaichi Nagata), mostly as a distributor of foreign titles. They were somehow involved with, of all things, the production of the 1988 slasher movie *Cheerleader Camp*. And by the 90s, they were able to produce films on their own once again... and it wasn't long before the Super Monster was back. But then, he wouldn't be a giant, super, or space monster; he would become the guardian of the universe.

Fans in the west have reacted to *Super Monster* as something they might have dragged in on their shoe. But then again, most of them do not seem to be the target audience. I do not gain anything by listening to 30 or 40-year-old men complaining that a movie made for 10-year-olds plays like a movie made for 10-year-olds. Regardless, *Super Monster* is often derided as the worst of the worst, an especially short-sighted declaration. No one is ever going to make the argument that *Gamera, Super Monster* is a good movie. But it at least is not a *boring* one. The first monster shows up around 20 minutes into the film and a new one comes in usually ten minutes after that. In between, you get a quartet of lovely alien babes to gawk at. And Shunsuke Kikuchi's score is far and away better than the film deserves. There's no accounting for taste, but digging into *Super Monster* using the same criteria one would for a "normal" movie is the same as beating up a disabled person. *Super Monster* is a disabled movie, doomed from the get-go by its producer. But the filmmakers themselves did their damnedest to make the movie as best as they could, hamstringed such as they were. Considering the handicaps they had going into the project, they largely succeeded.

Perhaps my affinity for it stems from the fact that I was 11 years old when I saw the film, which was still within bounds of the movie's intended demographic. I saw *Super Monster* for the first time on a late-night showing on TBS in 1992. It was one of those things where you get the TV Guide in the newspaper on Sunday and see that it's on Saturday night, so you have to wait the whole week for it (something that never happens anymore with our streaming services). Nobody in the history of the universe was as hyped for *Super Monster* as I was. And when it finally came on, I enjoyed the living hell out of that thing. When they had the credits in outer space with the polka-style song, I was like "Hmm. Okay. This is gonna be a different kind of Gamera movie. 'Written by Niisan Takahashi; Directed by Noriaki Yuasa'? Okay, we're still in good hands."

So, all the monsters are dead and Gamera goes off to fight Zanon. I'm sitting there, watching them cut back and forth and I'm thinking "This is it. They're finally gonna do something! They've been building it all up to this. It's gotta be great!" And then cut to a lame optical explosion from the far distance. "Really? That's all?" And I was traumatized for a good long while after that. I certainly didn't appreciate that everybody was all happy after Gamera died. And the happy end titles music just felt like it was mocking me.

I do remember this as well; when I saw the movie in 1992, the voiceover announcer would say "We now return to *Guh-mare-uh*, *Super Monster* on TBS Nite Flix." When they re-ran the film in 1993, that same announcer then said "We now return to *Gamera, Super Monster* on TBS Nite Flix" correctly. At least they put some respect on his name.

But don't just take my word for it. Here are some other perspectives/hot takes about the movie.

"It was the last of the Gamera films that I saw. After everything I'd read, I was fully prepared for the worst, but found myself having fun with it and haven't regretted the several times I've revisited it since that time. There are certainly better movies and Gamera's demise is total BS, but the wacky, barebones story works surprisingly well and the repackaged action plays better than one might expect. It also boasts some of Shunsuke Kikuchi's best work. Yuasa really manages to make a little something out of nothing in terms of resources. It's a fun little picture and I rather enjoy it. In fact, I might just give it another spin soon." —Tyler E. Martin

"*Gamera, Super Monster* was my first Gamera movie and have fond memories of when I first saw it in Kindergarten. It was on local Channel 5's *World Beyond* program which mostly showed giant monster movies and at the end of each program, they'd announce next week's movie. This time it was "Gamera, Super Monster."

Never heard of Gamera before and for the next week I wondered what he'd look like (I originally imagined a mish-mash of Godzilla and King Kong). Skip to next week and by golly, I was *floored.* A jet-powered flying turtle with kick-ass theme music? Get out of here! I was lucky with my viewing cause this would be only the first I'd catch it till way later in high school where I think they showed it on TBS.

Anywho, *World Beyond* was notorious for hacking their movies to shreds to fit the time slot so unbeknownst to me, I never knew Gamera battled Guiron and Viras till way later. I'm thankful the Jiger fight remained intact since she'd go on to become my favorite Gamera kaiju (and movie, next to this one) and that I wouldn't be able to see it till college. I'm glad my first Gamera was this one because it introduced me to the essence of what he's all about and especially his rogue's gallery.

I still have the VHS tape of *Super Monster* my parents taped for me. It also contains my favorite score of the franchise. I think I'm the only other person who loves *Super Monster* out there, but man oh man, I never did like that ending." —David Silliman

"Even with all the suffering behind the scenes, I still adore this film. It feels like a kaiju movie set inside a little kid's brain which has now been damaged from overexposure to Hollywood blockbusters as well as manga and anime." —Patrick Macias

"It is by far the weirdest entry in the Gamera series, which is saying a lot because some of his movies are crazy. It's a cynical cash grab, but it has at least a smidgeon of heart." —Matt Ferrett, monstersconquertheworld.com

"Clip show movies, are often quite hated within the fan community. From a completely shallow perspective, it's easy to see why: the audience feels cheated at seeing recycled footage. I get it. But, as a creator, I also appreciate the challenge faced by the filmmakers (in addition to writing books, I made a few small films as a teenager, so I do understand that creative process as well). No one sets out to make a clip show movie because they want to. Almost always, unfortunate circumstances dictate the restrictive conditions and it's a truly unique challenge to make a movie based on existing footage!

Now, most fans will immediately compare *Gamera, Super Monster* to *Godzilla's Revenge*, but not me. To me, *Super Monster* is more evocative of *Game of Death* (1978) and *Trail of the Pink Panther* (1982). *Game of Death* was a movie Bruce Lee was shooting prior to *Enter the Dragon* (1973). He halted shooting to take part in the more lucrative Warner Bros production with plans to resume *Game of Death* once he finished. When Lee passed away unexpectedly, his footage from *Game of Death* was repurposed for a film of the same name, but with a totally different storyline—an inferior storyline I might add. Similarly, Peter Sellers had plans to do a last Pink Panther movie before he too unexpectedly died. And so series writer/director Blake Edwards mined an extensive group of outtakes from *The Pink Panther Strikes Again* (1976) and flashbacks from other past films to concoct the clip show-ish *Trail of the Pink Panther*. It's a film that I enjoy watching more so as a creator than as a casual viewer.

And that finally leads me to *Gamera, Super Monster*, the much-maligned entry of kaiju fandom. Though I don't positively love it, I appreciate it and I do enjoy viewings of it. As to why, there are a few reasons. As I said before, as a creator, I appreciated the challenge faced by Noriaki Yuasa and Niisan Takahashi in creating this feature. Though Gamera was a fictional character, in an abstract way like Peter Sellers and Bruce Lee, I feel that Gamera was indeed "dead" at the time period in which the film was made (and I certainly don't mean to make light of the deaths of Lee or Sellers, both of whom I am fans of). Godzilla was in retirement and in his absence, no giant monsters had appeared in Japanese films for several years (I'm not counting the two Japanese dinosaur movies of 1977: *Legend of Dinosaurs and Monster Birds* and *The Last Dinosaur*). But what made Gamera more "dead" than anything else was the lack of funds available. Due to the lack of a budget, there wasn't really any money for new Gamera scenes outside of the new flying scenes. So that's why I compare *Super Monster* more to *Game of Death* or *Trail of the Pink Panther* over *Godzilla's Revenge*. For what they had to work with, I truly appreciate the efforts of Yuasa and Takahashi.

On a more shallow level, I enjoy the film because it serves up the best of the Showa era's monster footage. Let's face it, there are times when I really want to watch *Gamera vs. Gyaos* again. And yet at the same time, I'm also not dying to see the film in its entirety—the whole road construction subplot, etc. The same can be said for many other Gamera entries. So sometimes when I get a hankering for Showa era Gamera, the best choice for me is *Super Monster.* Gamera's monster battles have always been undeniably interesting, after all, and seeing them all back-to-back is quite fun. And again, I appreciate how Yuasa and Takahashi managed to craft a story around the old footage. If I was to lodge one large complaint against the film, it wouldn't have anything to do with the story or the space heroines, I just wish Gamera had gotten a better death scene than an explosion far off in the distance. The fact that Gamera actually dies in one his Showa entry films is something of a milestone overall and I just wish they had the budget to give him a slightly grander final scene.

Other than that, *Super Monster* is another fascinating case study of filmmakers doing the best they could with what they had." —John LeMay, editor of *The Lost Films Fanzine*

In Japan, *Super Monster* doesn't have nearly the vitriol directed at it as it does in the west. There was a 40th anniversary screening in late 2020 that was attended by Mach Fumiake, in which she showed she could still do the spacewomen transformation gesturing. Fumiake seemed absolutely thrilled to be there. In fact, she's still being invited onto Japanese game shows or talk shows and asked to do the gesture miming. Thus far, however, she has not transformed into Kilara...

As for *Gamera, Super Monster*, despite what you or I or anyone else might think of its quality or lack thereof, I feel its truest legacy was described to me by a Japanese friend who saw it in its original 1980 theatrical release—"The crowd I saw it with thought it was fine. It did the job it was meant to do: entertain 10-year-olds."

Keep believin' in love for the future, Kilaras and Keiichis. Keep believin'.

APPENDIX

Mach Fumiake (Kilara) today, proving *Gamera, Super Monster* did in fact have a screenplay.

Yaeko Tajima (Marsha) today as pop singer Yaya.

Yoko Komatsu (Mitan) today.

Keiko Kudo (Giruge) today.

Koichi Maeda (Keiichi) today.

Toshie Takada (Keiichi's Mother) today.

Japanese newspaper ad coupling *Gamera, Super Monster* with Tsuburaya Productions' *Six Ultra Brothers vs. the Monster Army* (1979).

Mach Fumiake in full Kilara regalia with the new Gamera suit during live shows publicizing the film.

International poster ad for the Cannes Film Festival, brought to you by Shochiku Company, LTD.

French release poster, entitled *Gameka* [sic] *and the 3 Super Women*, and erroneously claiming the film to be in [Daiei]scope format.

German DVD cover as *Gamera's Fight Against Frankenstein's Monster.* The tagline reads, "...And fighting against all others terrifically!"

Australian daybill poster as *Super Monster* which, as far as anyone knows, is the only place the actual international version was ever released.

Polish release poster as *Super Monster*.

Turkish release poster as *Gamera, Flying Godzilla*, also erroneously claiming the film to be in scope format, but more importantly promising monster cast members of Toho Company, LTD.'s *Destroy All Monsters*, Angilas, Mothra, Gorosaurus, Baragon, and King Ghidorah. Perhaps the SY-3 is meant to be Zanon?

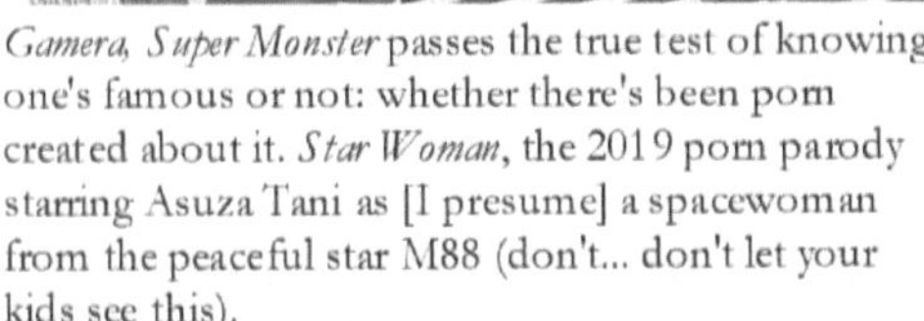

Gamera, Super Monster passes the true test of knowing one's famous or not: whether there's been porn created about it. *Star Woman*, the 2019 porn parody starring Asuza Tani as [I presume] a spacewoman from the peaceful star M88 (don't... don't let your kids see this).

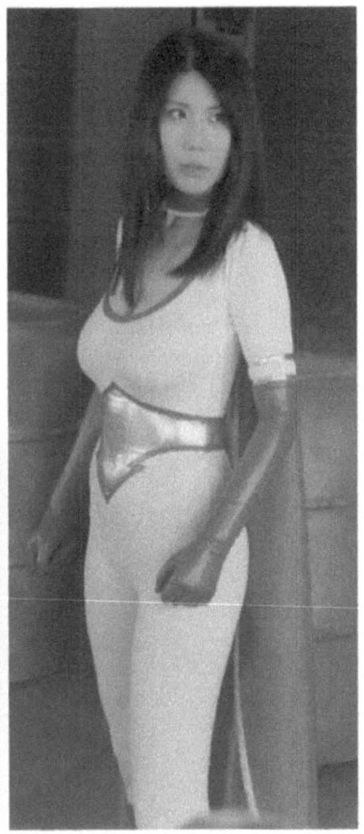

Gamera Decisive Battle Music File: Uchu Kaiju Gamera, thus far the only CD release of Shunsuke Kikuchi's full score for the film. Not included: the theme music from *Space Battleship Yamato* (for obvious reasons).

LP cover for the single release of *Love for Future*, sung by Mach Fumiake.

Noriaki Yuasa was a guest at G-Fest 2000 in Burbank, CA and out of nowhere, Mach Fumiake appeared. Photo courtesy Aaron Conway.

Left: Ad for 40th anniversary screening of *Super Monster* with Mach Fumiake in attendance. Above: Fumiake on stage about to transform into a spacewoman for an enthralled crowd.

GAMERA, SUPER MONSTER
宇宙怪獣ガメラ

Alternate titles: *Space Monster Gamera* (Japan*), Super Monster* (International), *Gameka and the 3 Super Women* (France), *Gamera, Flying Godzilla* (Turkey), *Robber Vessel Zanon* (Finland), *Gamera's Fight Against Frankenstein's Monster* (Germany)
Japanese release date: March 20th, 1980
U.S. release date: May 1980 (some sources claim 1981) on MTV by Filmways Pictures
Run time: 92 minutes (no print ever ran 109 minutes as some sources claim)
Shot in 1.85 standard widescreen and Vistavision

Director: Noriaki Yuasa / 湯浅憲明
Writer: Niisan Takahashi / 高橋二三
Special Effects: Noriaki Yuasa / 湯浅憲明 (and Kazufumi Fuji /藤井和文 & Yuzo Kaneko / 金子友三)
Music: Shunsuke Kikuchi / 菊池俊輔

Cast: Mach Fumiake / マッハ文朱 (Kilara / キララ), Yaeko Kojima / 小島八重子 [やや] (Marsha / マーシャ), Yoko Komatsu / 小松蓉子 (Mitan / ミータン), Keiko Kudo / 工藤啓子 (Giruge / ギルゲ), Koichi Maeda / 前田晃一 (Keiichi Kinoshita / 木下圭一), Toshie Takada / 高田敏江 (Keiichi's Mother / 圭一の母), Osamu Kobayashi / 小林修 (Zanon Captain / ザノンキャプテンの声), Hiroji Hayashi / 林博二 ("Bad Boy A" / 不良少年A), Tetsuaki Toyosumi / 豊隅哲明 ("Bad Boy B" / 不良少年B), Hideki

Kobayashi / 小林英樹 ("Bad Boy C" / 不良少年C), Koichi Takei / 武井 弘一 (Kameari Park Policeman / 亀有公園のお巡りさん), Kimio Tobita / 飛田喜美雄 (Driver / 運転手), Makoto Ikeda / 池田真 (Keiichi's Schoolyard Friend / 圭一の友達), Tadashi Nakamura / 中村正 (Japanese Narrator / ナレーター), Ted Thomas (English Dub Narrator), Toru Kawai / 河合徹 (Gamera / ガメラ)

Reiko Tajima of *Godzilla vs. Mechagodzilla* (1974) is not in the movie as is often erroneously reported [looking at you, IMDB].

Taglines
Japan: Clash of monster vs. huge spaceship! Thrilling and exciting special effects blockbuster! Finally, the strongest super monster of the universe has come!
International: The strongest in the universe! Gamera returns again! Entertaining! Spectacular! A fantasy of space!
Australia: A titanic struggle for supremacy as starship Zanon invades the planet earth!
Germany: ...And fighting against all others terrifically!
Turkey: Three superwomen in white on the big screen

Theme song: ***Love for Future* / 愛は未来へ…**
Lyrics: Hisashi Yama / やまひさし
Music: Shunsuke Kikuchi / 菊池俊輔
Singer: Mach Fumiake / マッハ文朱
Distributor: Minorphone Records / ミノルフォン・レコード

Japanese lyrics:	**English lyrics:**
Ginga o koete	A loud voice that
Sakenu koe	crosses the galaxy.
Ima koso	Now is the time,
Mamore	to protect
Kono chikyu!	this earth!
Tomodachi ga iru	Friends are here.
Nakama ga iru	Partners are here.
Yujo ga aru	Friendship is here.
Ai ga aru	Love is here.
Tatakae Gamera	Fight, Gamera
Hi o hake Gamera	Breathe fire, Gamera
Aisuru mono no tame ni yuke	Go for those you love
Aisuru mono no tame ni yuke...	Go for those you love...
[unused stanza]	[unused stanza]
Seigi wa tsuneni	Justice will always
Aku ni katsu.	triumph over evil.
Shinjite	Trust
Mamore	and protect
Kono chikyu.	this earth.
Tomodachi ga iru	Friends are here.
Mikata ga iru	Allies are here.
Hagemashi ga aru	Encouragement is here.
Chie ga aru	Wisdom is here.
Sora tobe Gamera	Jump into the sky, Gamera
Umi yuke Gamera	Go into the sea, Gamera
Aisuru mono no tame ni yuke	Go for those you love
Aisuru mono no tame ni yuke...	Go for those you love...
Mirai wa tsutsuku	The future continues
Hate mo naku.	endlessly.
Yuki de	Courageously
Mamore	protect
Kono chikyu.	this earth.
Tomodachi ga iru	Friends are here.
Bokura ga iru	We are here.
Shiawase ga iru	Happiness is here.
Yume ga aru	Dreams are here.
Tatakae Gamera	Fight, Gamera
Hi o hake Gamera	Breathe fire, Gamera
Aisuru mono no tame ni yuke	Go for those you love
Aisuru mono no tame ni yuke...	Go for those you love...

BIBLIOGRAPHY

Aeon. *The Gamera Chronicles: The History of Daiei Fantastic Movies, 1942-1996*, Tokyo, Japan, Takeshobo, 1996

Galbraith IV, Stuart. *Monsters Are Attacking Tokyo!*, Venice, CA, Feral House, 1998

Kikuchi, Shunsuke. *Gamera Decisive Battle Music File: Space Monster Gamera*, VAP-Inc Records, 1996

Pusateri, Richard. Audio Commentary. *Gamera, Super Monster*, Arrow Video, 2020.

Ragone, August. Audio Commentary. *Gamera vs. Barugon*, Shout! Factory LLC, 2010

Tokuma Shoten TV Land Special Color Graph: Space Monster Gamera. Tokyo, Japan, Tokuma Publishing, 1980

Uchu Kaiju Gamera Theatrical Program. Tokyo, Japan, Tokuma Publishing, 1980.

"宇宙怪獣ガメラ." *Japanese Wikipedia*, Wikipedia Foundation, 2021, https://ja.wikipedia.org/wiki/宇宙怪獣ガメラ

FICTION BOOKS IN THE CONSTANTINE FURMAN LIBRARY, ALL AVAILABLE AT AMAZON.COM WORLDWIDE.

A Greyer Shade of White

Damned Kids

Street Walkin' Man

A Specter Tale

Another Specter Tale

Constantine Furman's
The Life of Marta

A Specter Tale Continues

Giant Monster Farmarna

Farmarna's Monster Martial Law

Fire Bird: Monster of the Skies
Coming soon. Cover not finalized

A Specter Tale Concludes
Coming October 2021. Cover not finalized.

Dragora, the Monster Goddess
Coming late January 2022. Cover not finalized.

BOOKS BY JOHN LEMAY, ALL AVAILABLE AT AMAZON.COM WORLDWIDE.

THE BIG BOOK OF JAPANESE GIANT MONSTER MOVIES SERIES

The third edition of the book that started it all! Reviews over 100 tokusatsu films between 1954 and 1988. All the Godzilla, Gamera, and Daimajin movies made during the Showa era are covered plus lesser known fare like *Invisible Man vs. The Human Fly* (1957) and *Conflagration* (1975). Softcover (380 pp/5.83" X 8.27") Suggested Retail: $19.99 SBN:978-1-7341546 -4-1

This third edition reviews over 75 tokusatsu films between 1989 and 2019. All the Godzilla, Gamera, and Ultraman movies made during the Heisei era are covered plus independent films like *Reigo, King of the Sea Monsters* (2005), *Demeking, the Sea Monster* (2009) and *Attack of the Giant Teacher* (2019)! Softcover (260 pp/5.83" X 8.27") Suggested Retail: $19.99 ISBN: 978-1- 7347816-4-9

This second edition of the Rondo Award nominated book covers un-produced scripts like *Bride of Godzilla* (1955), partially shot movies like *Giant Horde Beast Nezura* (1963), and banned films like *Prophecies of Nostradamus* (1974), plus hundreds of other lost productions. Softcover/Hard-cover (470pp. /7" X 10") Suggested Retail: $24.99 (sc)/$39.95(hc)ISBN: 978-1-7341546-0-3 (hc)

This sequel to *The Lost Films* covers the non-giant monster unmade movie scripts from Japan such as *Frankenstein vs. the Human Vapor* (1963), *After Japan Sinks* (1974-76), plus lost movies like *Fearful Attack of the Flying Saucers* (1956) and *Venus Flytrap* (1968). Hardcover (200 pp/5.83" X 8.27")/Softcover (216 pp/ 5.5" X 8.5") Suggested Retail: $9.99 (sc)/$24.99(hc) ISBN:978-1-7341546 -3-4 (hc)

This companion book to *The Lost Films* charts the development of all the prominent Japanese monster movies including discarded screenplays, story ideas, and deleted scenes. Also includes bios for writers like Shinichi Sekizawa, Niisan Takahashi and many others. Comprehensive script listing and appendices as well. Hardcover/Softcover (370 pp./ 6"X9") Suggested Retail: $16.95(sc)/$34.99(hc)ISBN: 978-1-7341546-5-8 (hc)

Examines the differences between the U.S. and Japanese versions of over 50 different tokusatsu films like *Gojira* (1954)/*Godzilla, King of the Monsters!* (1956), *Gamera* (1965)/ *Gammera, the Invincible* (1966), *Submersion of Japan* (1973)/*Tidal Wave* (1975), and many, many more! Softcover (540 pp./ 6"X9") Suggested Retail: $22.99(sc) ISBN: 978-1-953221-77-3

This second volume examines the differences between the European and Japanese versions of tokusatsu films including the infamous "Cozzilla" colorized version of *Godzilla, King of the Monsters!* from 1977, plus rarities like *Terremoto 10 Grado*, the Italian cut of *Legend of Dinosaurs*. The book also examines the condensed Champion Matsuri edits of Toho's effects films. Coming 2022.

HUMOR

Throughout the 1960s and 1970s the Italian film industry cranked out over 600 "Spaghetti Westerns" and for every *Fistful of Dollars* were a dozen pale imitations, some of them hilarious. Many of these lesser known Spaghettis are available in bargain bin DVD packs and stream for free online. If ever you've wondered which are worth your time and which aren't, this is the book for you. Softcover (160pp./5.06" X 7.8") Suggested Retail: $9.99

The End

www.ingramcontent.com/pod-product-compliance
Ingram Content Group UK Ltd.
Pitfield, Milton Keynes, MK11 3LW, UK
UKHW040031200726
13854UKWH00001B/468

9 798522 013776